9/11 0x

CR ✓

D0520507

Team Spirit

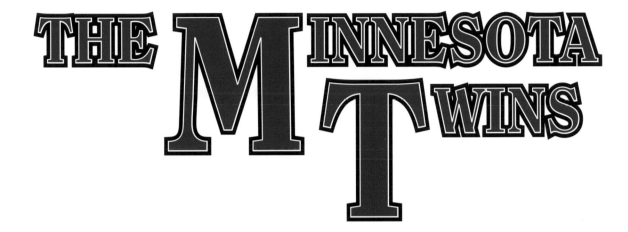

THE MINNESOTA TWINS

BY
MARK STEWART

Content Consultant
James L. Gates, Jr.
Library Director
National Baseball Hall of Fame and Museum

NORWOOD HOUSE PRESS
CHICAGO, ILLINOIS

Norwood House Press
P.O. Box 316598
Chicago, Illinois 60631

For information regarding Norwood House Press, please visit our website at:
www.norwoodhousepress.com or call 866-565-2900.

All photos courtesy of AP Images—AP/Wide World Photos, Inc. except the following:
Polar Bear (6); Fatima (6); F.W. Rueckheim & Brother (7); Topps, Inc. (7, 9 top, 14, 21, 28, 30, 35
left, 37, 40 top & 43); Exhibit Supply Company (16 & 17); John Klein (18);
Author's Collection (20 & 34 top); Black Book archives: (22, 31, 35 top & 41 top);
Sweet Caporal (34 left); Sports Stars Publishing (40 bottom).
Special thanks to Topps, Inc.

Editor: Mike Kennedy
Designer: Ron Jaffe
Project Management: Black Book Partners, LLC.
Special thanks to Dan Neumann, Julia Neumann, Rob Wiste and Wendy Woodfill.

Library of Congress Cataloging-in-Publication Data

Stewart, Mark, 1960-
    The Minnesota Twins / by Mark Stewart ; with consultant
James L. Gates, Jr.
        p. cm. -- (Team spirit)
    Summary: "Presents the history, accomplishments and key personalities of
the Minnesota Twins baseball team. Includes timelines, quotes, maps,
glossary and websites"--Provided by publisher.
    Includes bibliographical references and index.
    ISBN-13: 978-1-59953-058-1 (library edition : alk. paper)
    ISBN-10: 1-59953-058-9 (library edition : alk. paper)
    1. Minnesota Twins (Baseball team)--History--Juvenile literature. I.
Gates, Jr., James L. II. Title. III. Series: Stewart, Mark, 1960- Team
spirit.
    GV875.M55S74 2007
    796.357'6409776579--dc22
                                            2006015329

COVER PHOTO: Lew Ford is congratulated by his teammates after
hitting a home run against the Oakland A's in 2005.

Table of Contents

SPORTS WORDS & VOCABULARY WORDS: In this book, you will find many words that are new to you. You may also see familiar words used in new ways. The glossary on page 46 gives the meanings of baseball words, as well as "everyday" words that have special baseball meanings. These words appear in **bold type** throughout the book. The glossary on page 47 gives the meanings of vocabulary words that are not related to baseball. They appear in ***bold italic type*** throughout the book.

Meet the Twins

Every baseball team is known for some special quality that sets it apart from other teams. The Minnesota Twins are known for their great hitting *tradition*. Ever since the Twins began playing in Minnesota, they have specialized in filling their **lineup** with dangerous hitters. Over the years, their stars have often been among the leaders in hits, home runs, batting average and **runs batted in (RBIs)**.

Minnesota fans know there is more to the Twins than hitting. They win with slick defense, smart base-running, and good pitching. The Twins may not have the *swagger* of some teams, but they know what it takes to play nine innings of winning baseball.

This book tells the story of the Twins. They are a team named after two cities, with a fan following that spans five states. They have a long history and an exciting future, and they have been at the center of some of baseball's most amazing—and heartwarming—stories.

Luis Castillo, Joe Mauer, and Luis Rodriquez
jump for joy after a game-winning hit.

Way Back When

The Twins trace their history back to 1901, which was the first year of the **American League (A.L.)**. The team was called the Senators, and they played in Washington, D.C. Their greatest star in those early years was Walter Johnson, a **sidearm** pitcher who threw

JOHNSON, WASHINGTON

the ball close to 100 miles per hour. Another important person in the team's history was Clark Griffith. He began as the manager and ended up owning the team.

The Senators won the **World Series** in 1924, and also won the A.L. **pennant** in 1925 and 1933. They had some very good players over the years, including Goose Goslin, Joe Cronin, Heinie Manush, George Case, and Mickey Vernon. However, most seasons, the Senators were not a successful team. In fact, a popular joke was that Washington was "first in war, first in peace—and *last* in the American League."

By the 1950s, Griffith's nephew, Calvin, had taken

Second Row: Hughes, Schaefer, Morgan, Manager Griffith, Milan, Shanks, Moeller, Groom. Sitting: Mullin, Calvo, Foster, Altrock, Ainsmith, Laporte, Acosta, Williams.

Martin, Trainer Henry Harper Boehling Gandil Johnson McBride Engle Gideon Gallia

charge of the team. The Senators were losing a lot of games, and losing a lot of money. Several baseball-starved cities offered to give the team a new home. Louisville, Houston, Dallas, Toronto, Los Angeles, and San Francisco all wanted a team. In the end, the state of Minnesota won over the Griffith family. The team

GRIFFITH, Washington - Americans

moved to the city of Bloomington in 1961, and played in brand new Metropolitan Stadium. They would *represent* the entire state, but took their name from the nearby "twin cities" of Minneapolis and St. Paul, and became the Twins.

The Twins brought some very good players from Washington. Jim Kaat and Camilo Pascual were among the best pitchers in the A.L., while **sluggers** Harmon Killebrew and Bob Allison led the batting attack. By 1965, the

MINNESOTA TWINS

Twins had a lineup that also included Zoilo Versalles, Tony Oliva, Jim Perry, and Mudcat Grant. That season, they won 102 games and reached the World Series.

TOP LEFT: Walter Johnson   **TOP RIGHT**: Clark Griffith
BOTTOM LEFT: The 1913 Senators
BOTTOM RIGHT: 50 years later—the 1963 Minnesota Twins.

The Twins were known as one of the hardest-hitting teams in baseball. In 1967, Killebrew and Oliva were joined by Rod Carew. He would win seven batting championships with the Twins. In the 1970s, top players Bert Blyleven, Bill Campbell, Butch Wynegar, and Roy Smalley also wore the Minnesota uniform. Despite these stars, the team went more than 20 seasons without winning another pennant. Many blamed Calvin Griffith, who was unwilling to pay his players high *salaries*.

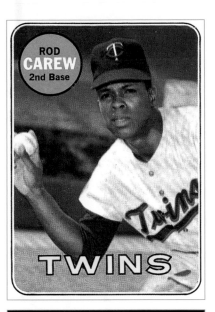

Finally, in 1987, the Twins returned to the World Series. Led by Frank Viola, Kent Hrbek, Gary Gaetti, and Kirby Puckett, they became champions for the first time since moving to Minnesota. In 1991, the Twins won it all again.

After these championships, the Twins suffered through several losing seasons. In 2002, Major League Baseball considered *eliminating* the

Twins, or getting their owner to sell or move the team. For a brief moment, no one knew whether the Twins would survive!

LEFT: Harmon Killerbrew
TOP: Rod Carew   **BOTTOM**: Kirby Puckett and Frank Viola

The Team Today

Just when things looked their worst for the Twins, the team started winning. Led by Torii Hunter, Eric Milton, Brad Radke, Jacque Jones, Doug Mientkiewicz, and Johan Santana, Minnesota became one of baseball's toughest teams. New manager Ron Gardenhire taught his young stars to play like **veterans**. All talk of eliminating the team ended. Instead, fans got excited about the Twins again.

In 2002, the Twins won 94 games and finished first in the A.L. **Central Division**. They defeated the Oakland A's in the **playoffs** and reached the **American League Championship Series (ALCS)**. They lost to the Anaheim Angels four games to one, and missed a chance to return to the World Series.

The Twins were A.L. Central champions again in 2003 and 2004, and have been playing good, winning baseball ever since. Although the fans are happy that the Twins are back to their winning ways, the players will not rest until they can hold up another World Series trophy.

Shannon Stewart and Joe Mauer exchange "high fives."

Home Turf

Since 1982, the Twins have played in the Hubert H. Humphrey Metrodome, which was named after Minnesota's beloved Senator. Although it looks large from the outside, the Metrodome is actually small as **major-league** ballparks go. That explains why it gets so noisy when big crowds start cheering and waving their "Homer Hankies."

When the Metrodome opened, two things made it very unusual. The *artificial* playing surface was so springy that a short hit sometimes bounced right over the outfielder's head and rolled to the wall. Also, a section of 7,600 seats for football games was designed to be *retractable* for baseball. They pulled back over the right field fence and were covered by a huge black *tarpaulin*, which fans sometimes call the "Trash Bag."

THE METRODOME BY THE NUMBERS

- There are 45,423 seats in the Metrodome.
- The first game in the Metrodome was played on April 6, 1982. The Twins lost to the Seattle Mariners 11–7.
- The "Trash Bag" in right field is 23 feet high.
- The distance from home plate to the left field foul pole is 343 feet.
- The distance from home plate to the center field fence is 408 feet.
- The distance from home plate to the right field foul pole is 327 feet.

The Metrodome is packed for a tribute to Kirby Puckett. The most-loved Twin died in 2006.

Dressed for Success

The first uniforms worn by the Twins in 1961 were almost identical to the ones they wore in Washington in 1960. The team colors were white with scarlet and navy blue, while the team name was written in slanted script across the chest. The home uniforms featured **pinstripes** and the road uniforms were a bluish gray. The caps had an interlocking T and C, which stood for Twin Cities. The Twins did not want to use the letter M because fans might think it only stood for Minneapolis. A patch on the sleeve showed the team's new **logo**—twin baseball players from Minneapolis and St. Paul shaking hands across the Mississippi River.

During the 1970s and 1980s, the Twins switched to a modern-looking uniform. They went back to a more traditional style in 1987 and won their first championship. That season they also replaced the TC on their caps with the letter M. Today, the Twins continue to wear their classic-looking uniforms in most games. They also returned to the TC cap logo.

Rich Rollins poses in the Twins' pinstriped uniform of the 1960s. The team logo can be seen on his sleeve.

14

UNIFORM BASICS

The baseball uniform has not changed much since the Senators began playing. It has four main parts:

- a cap or batting helmet with a sun visor;
- a top with a player's number on the back;
- pants that reach down between the ankle and the knee;
- stirrup-style socks.

The uniform top sometimes has a player's name on the back. The team's name, city, or logo is usually on the front. Baseball teams wear light-colored uniforms when they play at home, and darker styles when they play on the road.

For more than 100 years, baseball uniforms were made of wool *flannel* and were very baggy. This helped the sweat *evaporate* and gave players the freedom to move around. Today's uniforms are made of *synthetic* fabrics that stretch with players and keep them dry and cool.

Pitcher Carlos Silva wears one of the team's current uniforms. It looks very much like the uniform of the 1960s.

We Won!

The Twins won the World Series in 1987 and 1991. In both of these victories, they trailed three games to two, but were able to come back and win in seven games. The team's first championship—when they played as the Washington Senators—was also an unforgettable comeback.

The year was 1924, and their opponents were the New York Giants. The Senators were hoping their 36-year-old star, Walter Johnson, would pitch them to victory. But he lost Game One and Game Five, and the Giants took a three games to two lead in the series. Tom Zachary won Game Six for Washington 2–1, setting up a thrilling Game Seven.

Walter P. Johnson
PITCHER, WASHINGTON, AM. L.

The two teams battled through seven innings and the Giants held a 3–1 lead. The Senators loaded the bases with two out in the eighth, and player-manager Bucky Harris came to the plate. He hit a grounder to third, and it looked like Washington had wasted its last chance. But

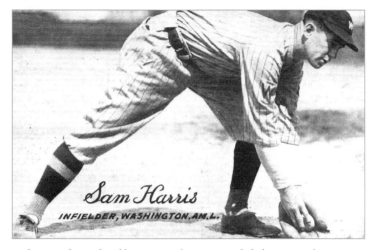

luck was on the Senators' side—the ball struck a pebble and bounced high over the fielder's head. Two runners scored and the game eventually went into **extra innings** tied 3–3. Harris called in Johnson to stop the Giants, and this time he did. In the 12th inning, Earl McNeeley hit a double and Muddy Ruel crossed home plate with the championship-winning run.

Sixty-three years later, in 1987, the Twins once again found themselves trailing in the World Series, three games to two—this time to the St. Louis Cardinals. In Game Six, Kent Hrbek got the big hit for Minnesota. He hit a **grand slam** to help the Twins win 11–5. In Game Seven, with the crowd noise almost *deafening*, Frank Viola held the Cardinals to two runs with help from **reliever** Jeff Reardon. The Twins scratched out single runs in four different innings to win 4–2, and bring Minnesota its first championship.

LEFT: Walter Johnson warms up before a game.
ABOVE: Bucky Harris fields a grounder. His hit in the 1924 World Series helped the team win Game Seven.

The 1991 World Series was even more exciting. In fact, it was one of the best ever played. The Twins had added **All-Star** pitcher Jack Morris to their team, and he beat the Atlanta Braves in Game One. The Twins won the next game on a dramatic eighth-inning home run, but the Braves did not quit. They won the next three, and took a three games to two lead.

The Twins *recovered* to win Game Six 4–3. It lasted 11 innings, and ended on a dramatic home run by Kirby Puckett. Puckett had a hand in every Minnesota run, and made one of the best catches in World Series history, too.

The next day, in Game Seven, Morris and Atlanta's John Smoltz pitched one scoreless inning after another. As the game wore on, it became clear that whichever team managed to cross home plate first would be the world champion. Once again, the game went into extra innings. Never before had the final World Series game gone so long without a run.

Manager Tom Kelly told Morris that he wanted to take him out, but the exhausted pitcher refused. Morris held the Braves in

the top of the 10th inning, then watched as teammate Dan Gladden hit a **bloop double** to start the bottom of the 10th. Chuck Knoblauch bunted Gladden to third, then the Braves loaded the bases to create a **force-out** at any base. Kelly sent **pinch-hitter** Gene Larkin to the plate. With the fans on the edge of their seats, Larkin hit a single to give the Twins the championship.

LEFT: Tom Kelly, the popular manager who led the Twins to two championships. **ABOVE**: Jack Morris pitches in the 1991 World Series.

19

Go-To Guys

To be a true star in baseball, you need more than a quick bat and a strong arm. You have to be a "go-to guy"—someone the manager wants on the pitcher's mound or in the batter's box when it matters most. Twins (and Senators) fans have had a lot to cheer about over the years, including these great stars...

THE PIONEERS

WALTER JOHNSON   Pitcher

• BORN: 11/6/1887   • DIED: 12/10/1946   • PLAYED FOR TEAM: 1907 TO 1927

Walter Johnson threw his legendary fastball with a whipping motion that made it very difficult to see. He led the A.L. in strikeouts 12 times and was one of the first players voted into the **Hall of Fame.**

"Goose" Goslin
"SENATORS"
FIELDER, WASHINGTON A. L.

GOOSE GOSLIN   Outfielder

• BORN: 10/16/1900   • DIED: 5/15/1971
• PLAYED FOR TEAM: 1921 TO 1930, 1933 & 1938

Goose Goslin was one of the best **clutch hitters** of the 1920s and 1930s. He led the A.L. with a .379 average in 1928, and was a star on all three of Washington's World Series teams.

HARMON KILLEBREW
First Baseman/ Third Baseman/Outfielder

- BORN: 6/29/1936   • PLAYED FOR TEAM: 1954 TO 1974

Harmon Killebrew was the best player the Twins brought from Washington when they moved in 1961. One of history's most feared sluggers, he was an All-Star 10 times between 1961 and 1971, and was the A.L. **Most Valuable Player (MVP)** in 1969.

TONY OLIVA   Outfielder

- BORN: 7/20/1940
- PLAYED FOR TEAM: 1962 TO 1976

Tony Oliva won the batting championship in his first two full seasons with the Twins, and led the league in hits five times. A terrible knee injury cut short his *remarkable* career.

ROD CAREW   Second Baseman/ First Baseman

- BORN: 10/1/1945
- PLAYED FOR TEAM: 1967 TO 1978

Rod Carew was one of the smartest batters in history. He could hit any pitch hard, and place the ball wherever he pleased. Carew won seven batting championships with the Twins, including six from 1972 to 1978.

LEFT: Goose Goslin   **ABOVE**: Tony Oliva

MODERN STARS

KENT HRBEK — First Baseman

- BORN: 5/21/1960   • PLAYED FOR TEAM: 1981 TO 1994

Kent Hrbek was an enormous power hitter who scared opposing pitchers with his home run swing. He was quick and **sure-handed** in the field, making him one of the Twins' best **all-around** players.

GARY GAETTI — Third Baseman

- BORN: 8/19/1958
- PLAYED FOR TEAM: 1981 TO 1990

Gary Gaetti was a powerful hitter and a **Gold Glove** fielder, but his biggest contribution was his leadership. With Gaetti on the team, the Twins always felt they had a chance.

FRANK VIOLA — Pitcher

- BORN: 4/19/1960   • PLAYED FOR TEAM: 1982 TO 1989

Frank Viola was the player who showed the Twins how to win in the 1980s. The big left-hander was smooth and confident on the mound. He led the A.L. with 24 victories in 1988.

ABOVE: Gary Gaetti   **RIGHT**: Johan Santana

KIRBY PUCKETT   Outfielder

- BORN: 3/14/1961   • DIED: 3/6/2006   • PLAYED FOR TEAM: 1984 TO 1995

Kirby Puckett was the most beloved player in Twins history. He led the A.L. in hits four times, won a batting title, and was a hero in two World Series. Puckett began his career as a singles hitter, but over the years he learned how to use his powerful body to hit home runs.

JOHAN SANTANA   Pitcher

- BORN: 3/13/1979
- FIRST YEAR WITH TEAM: 2000

Johan Santana was discovered by the Twins while pitching in the **minor leagues** for the Houston Astros. After adding a **changeup** to his blazing fastball, he became one of the best left-handers in the league.

JOE MAUER   Catcher

- BORN: 4/19/1983
- FIRST YEAR WITH TEAM: 2004

Joe Mauer was the first player picked in the 2001 **draft**. Four years later, people were calling him one of the best all-around catchers in baseball.

On the Sidelines

More than any other team, the Twins prefer to hire their managers "from within." This means that they look inside their own *organization* for coaches and ex-players who have served the team well. This idea started back when the team played in Washington.

In 1924, a clever 27-year-old second baseman named Bucky Harris was asked to manage the Senators. He led the team to the pennant that season, and again in 1925. Harris also managed the team in the 1930s, 1940s, and 1950s. Other players who went on to manage the team included Ossie Bluege, Sam Mele, and Billy Martin.

In 1986, the Twins asked coach Tom Kelly to manage the team. He was unknown to most fans, but the players loved his relaxed style and teaching skills. In 1987 and again in 1991, he led the Twins to the championship. After Kelly retired in 2002, the Twins made his trusted coach, Ron Gardenhire, their new manager. Gardenhire led the team to first-place finishes in each of his first three seasons.

Ron Gardenhire, the manager Tom Kelly chose to follow in his footsteps.

One Great Day

No one knew what to expect when the 1991 World Series began. The Twins and Atlanta Braves had both finished last in 1990, and now—against all odds—they were playing for the championship. The Twins won the first two games, and then the Braves won the next three. Minnesota fans were confident their team could come back. After all, in 1987 the Twins had been in the same position against the St. Louis Cardinals and had won Games Six and Seven.

The players were confident, too. Before Game Six, Kirby Puckett made an announcement in the Minnesota locker room. "Jump on board, boys," he said. "I'm going to carry us tonight. Just back me up a little and I'll take us to Game Seven!"

Puckett was true to his word. He drove in one run and scored another early in the game. Then, with the score tied 2–2, he raced to the fence and made a fantastic leaping catch to rob Ron Gant of an extra-base hit. Moments later, Puckett drove in his team's third run. The Braves were able to tie the game and it went into extra innings.

Kirby Puckett celebrates his World Series home run against the Braves.

The Twins failed to score in the 10th inning. Their chances seemed to be running out. It was time for "Puck" to be a hero again.

Puckett **led off** the 11th inning against pitcher Charlie Leibrandt. He waited for the veteran to make a mistake, and when he saw the pitch he wanted, he drove a long home run into the left field seats to win the game 4–3. The next day, the Twins and Braves went into extra innings again. Minnesota won 1–0 for the championship.

Legend Has It

HARMON KILLEBREW

Was Harmon Killebrew the worst bunter in baseball history?

LEGEND HAS IT that he was. Killebrew batted nearly 10,000 times, yet he never made a sacrifice bunt. Of course, being a slugger, he was rarely asked to do so. But no one in history played as long as Killebrew without at least one successful bunt.

Which team has used a public address announcer the longest?

LEGEND HAS IT that the Twins have. Back in 1902, when they were the Washington Senators, the team hired a man named E. Lawrence Phillips to call out the lineups to fans before each game. Phillips used a cardboard *megaphone* so he could be heard.

Which Twin did pitchers hate to face when they were trying for a no-hitter?

LEGEND HAS IT that it was Zoilo Versalles. Rod Carew and Tony Oliva may have won batting championships for Minnesota, but it was their teammate, Versalles, who had a reputation for breaking up **no-hitters**. Four times during his career, he had the only hit for his team during a game.

LEFT: Harmon Killebrew   **ABOVE**: Zoilo Versalles

It Really Happened

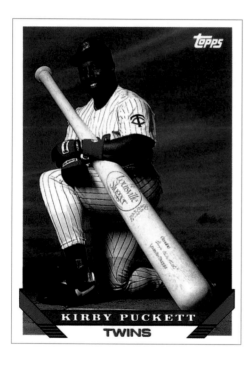

KIRBY PUCKETT
TWINS

In his first two years as a major leaguer, Kirby Puckett hit a grand total of four home runs. His teammates often teased him, claiming he was too weak to reach the fences. Finally, in 1986, Puckett had heard enough. While the other Twins watched in awe, he smashed 10 balls in a row into the left field seats during batting practice. That season, he went on to hit 31 home runs.

The following spring, at the Twins' training camp in Orlando, Florida, Puckett continued to work on his home run swing. He got into a good rhythm one day and began hitting ball after ball far over the left field fence. Suddenly, a policeman hopped onto the field and ran toward Puckett. He ordered him to stop.

He explained that Puckett's long home runs were destroying the cars parked at a nearby tractor-pull. When the Twins refused to stop their practice, the officer turned to the Twins' star and said, "If you swing that bat one more time, you're going to jail!"

Puckett's jaw dropped. Arrested for hitting home runs? Can he really *do* that?

The Twins did not want to find out. They agreed to hold batting practice in a covered cage, but for Puckett the damage was done. When he started hitting again, he could not concentrate. "Do you believe this," he complained. "The cop makes me stop hitting just when I was getting in a groove!"

LEFT: Kirby Puckett was known for his big bat—but not *this* big!
RIGHT: Puckett strides into a pitch.

Team Spirit

When the Twins are winning and the Metrodome is packed with screaming fans, there are few places in sports where it is harder to hear. Minnesota fans can almost see their energy *surge* through the players. The Twins have said many times that having their fans pulling for them is like having an "extra player" on the field.

Minnesota fans are not just famous for being loud. They are famous for being proud. Many bring special "Homer Hankies" to the game, and wave them back and forth when the team needs a home run. During the 1987 and 1991 World Series, there were so many bright white Homer Hankies being waved that it was almost blinding.

After 2001, when there was a chance that Minnesota might lose its team, the fans formed an extra-special bond with the Twins. They have come to understand that their club cannot always afford to put superstars on the field. All they ask is that their players give everything they have—when they do, the fans treat them like kings. In 2006, the Twins got great news. They would not only stay in Minnesota, a new ball park was being planned for the future!

Minnesota fans wave their "Homer Hankies."

Timeline

1924
The Senators defeat the New York Giants to win their only World Series.

1961
The team moves to Minnesota and becomes the Twins.

1965
The Twins win the pennant, but lose to the Los Angeles Dodgers in the World Series.

1901
The Washington Senators are one of eight teams in the new American League.

1964
Tony Oliva is named **Rookie of the Year** and wins the batting championship.

Walter Johnson, the team's first great star.

JOHNSON, WASHINGTON

Tony Oliva swings the silver bat he received for winning the batting championship.

Kent Hrbek, who hit a grand slam in the 1987 World Series.

1982
The Twins move into the Metrodome.

1987
The Twins defeat the St. Louis Cardinals to win the World Series.

1978
Rod Carew wins his seventh batting championship.

1991
The Twins defeat the Atlanta Braves to win the World Series.

2004
Johan Santana wins the A.L. **Cy Young Award**.

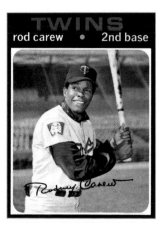

Rod Carew

Johan Santana shows the fans his Cy Young Award.

Fun Facts

NAME OF THE GAME

Every player on the Twins has a special nickname only his teammates use. This tradition was started in the late 1990s by outfielder Torii Hunter. Hunter was nicknamed "Spidey" because of the way he could climb the outfield walls like Spiderman trying to catch home runs.

INSIDE BASEBALL

Game One of the 1987 World Series—played in the Metrodome—was the first World Series game ever held indoors.

BLAST FROM THE PAST

In 1967, Harmon Killebrew smashed a home run 530 feet into the upper deck at Metropolitan Stadium. The ball was hit so hard that it splintered two seats. They were painted orange and no one was allowed to sit in them again.

ABOVE: Torii Hunter climbs the outfield wall.   **RIGHT**: Jim Kaat

DOING IT ALL

During the 1960s, Cesar Tovar was the Twins' "do-it-all" player. On September 22, 1968, he really *did* do it all—he played all nine positions in the same game! When Tovar took the pitcher's mound, one of the batters he faced was slugger Reggie Jackson. Incredibly, he struck Jackson out.

LONG LASTING

Of all the members of the 1961 Twins, pitcher Jim Kaat played the longest, 24 years. He was also one of the only people ever to pitch in four different **decades**. Kaat started with the Senators in 1959 and finished with the Cardinals in 1983.

FAN-TASTIC

The Twins are the "home team" for millions of fans in the upper Midwest. Look in the stadium parking lot and you will see license plates from Minnesota, Wisconsin, North Dakota, South Dakota, and Iowa. Many fans from Canada also make the long trip south to watch the Twins.

Talking Baseball

"I wanted to be a big leaguer more than anything else. I thought baseball players were the most wonderful people in the world."
—*Harmon Killebrew, on his childhood dream*

"If you believe in yourself, you will succeed. Hey man, that's what it takes to be a winner and become the best you can be."
—*Kirby Puckett, on always staying positive*

"The baseball fan who comes into our parks should always be sure that he's watching the same game he played as a boy."
    —*Clark Griffith, on why the rules of baseball should not be changed*

"When I see that little white ball go up, I want to catch it, no matter what. If I have to knock myself silly doing it, so be it."
    —*Torii Hunter, on how he makes so many great catches*

"Hitting is an art, not an exact science."
    —*Rod Carew, on batting against major-league pitching*

"You can't hit what you can't see."
    —*Walter Johnson, on why it was so hard to hit his fastball*

LEFT: Harmon Killebrew and Kirby Puckett meet at an old-timers event.   **ABOVE**: Torii Hunter shows off the Gold Glove he won as the league's best center fielder.

For the Record

The great Twins (and Senators) teams and players have left their marks on the record books. These are the "best of the best"…

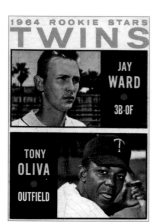

Tony Oliva

Bill Campbell

TWINS AWARD WINNERS

WINNER	AWARD	YEAR
Albie Pearson*	Rookie of the Year	1958
Bob Allison*	Rookie of the Year	1959
Tony Oliva	Rookie of the Year	1964
Zoilo Versalles	Most Valuable Player	1965
Rod Carew	Rookie of the Year	1967
Harmon Killebrew	Most Valuable Player	1969
Jim Perry	Cy Young Award	1970
Bill Campbell	Reliever of the Year	1976
Rod Carew	Most Valuable Player	1977
John Castino	Co-Rookie of the Year	1979
Frank Viola	World Series Most Valuable Player	1987
Frank Viola	Cy Young Award	1988
Chuck Knoblauch	Rookie of the Year	1991
Tom Kelly	Manager of the Year	1991
Jack Morris	World Series Most Valuable Player	1991
Marty Cordova	Rookie of the Year	1995
Johan Santana	Cy Young Award	2004

Member of the Washington Senators

TWINS ACHIEVEMENTS

ACHIEVEMENT	YEAR
A.L. Pennant Winners*	1924
World Series Champions*	1924
A.L. Pennant Winners*	1925
A.L. Pennant Winners*	1933
A.L. Pennant Winners	1965
A.L. West Champions	1969
A.L. West Champions	1970
A.L. West Champions	1987
A.L. Pennant Winners	1987
World Series Champions	1987
A.L. West Champions	1991
A.L. Pennant Winners	1991
World Series Champions	1991
A.L. Central Champions	2002
A.L. Central Champions	2003
A.L. Central Champions	2004

Washington Senators

TOP: John Castino, the 1979 Co-Rookie of the Year.
ABOVE: Kirby Puckett greets Kent Hrbek after his grand slam in the 1987 World Series.
LEFT: The Twins celebrate after winning the 1965 A.L. pennant.

Pinpoints

T he history of a baseball team is made up of many smaller stories. These stories take place all over the map—not just in the city a team calls "home." Match the push-pins on these maps to the Team Facts and you will begin to see the story of the Twins unfold!

TEAM FACTS

1   Minneapolis, Minnesota—*The Twins have played here since 1982. They played in nearby Bloomington from 1961 to 1981.*

2   Chicago, Illinois—*Kirby Puckett was born here.*

3   Zeeland, Michigan—*Jim Kaat was born here.*

4   Hempstead, New York—*Frank Viola was born here.*

5   Washington, D.C.—*The team played here as the Senators from 1901 to 1960.*

Bert Blyleven

6   Pine Bluff, Arkansas—*Torii Hunter was born here.*

7   Houston, Texas—*Chuck Knoblauch was born here.*

8   Payette, Idaho—*Harmon Killebrew was born here.*

9   Pinar del Rio, Cuba—*Tony Oliva was born here.*

10 Gatun, Panama Canal Zone—*Ron Carew was born here.*

11 Tovar Merida, Venezuela—*Johan Santana was born here.*

12 Zeist, Netherlands—*Bert Blyleven was born here.*

Play Ball

Baseball is a game played between two teams over nine innings. Teams take one turn at bat and one turn in the field during each inning. A turn at bat ends when three outs are made. The batters on the hitting team try to reach base safely. The players on the fielding team try to prevent this from happening.

In baseball, the ball is controlled by the pitcher. The pitcher must throw the ball to the batter, who decides whether or not to swing at each pitch. If a batter swings and misses, it is a strike. If the batter lets a good pitch go by, it is also a strike. If the batter swings and the ball does not stay in fair territory (between the v-shaped lines that begin at home plate) it is called "foul," and is counted as a strike. If the pitcher throws three strikes, the batter is out. If the pitcher throws four bad pitches before that, the batter is awarded first base. This is called a base-on-balls, or "walk."

When the batter swings the bat and hits the ball, everyone springs into action. If a fielder catches a batted ball before it hits the ground, the batter is out. If a fielder scoops the ball off the ground and throws it to first base before the batter arrives, the batter is out. If the batter reaches first base safely, he is credited with a hit. A one-base hit is called a single, a two-base hit is called a double, a three-base hit is called a triple, and a four-base hit is called a home run.

Runners who reach base are only safe when they are touching one of the bases. If they are caught between the bases, the fielders can tag them with the ball and record an out.

A batter who is able to circle the bases and make it back to home plate before three outs are made is credited with a run scored. The team with the most runs after nine innings is the winner.

Anyone who has played baseball (or softball) knows that it can be a complicated game. Every player on the field has a job to do. Different players have different strengths and weaknesses. The pitchers, batters, and managers make hundreds of decisions every game. The more you play and watch baseball, the more "little things" you are likely to notice. The next time you are at a game, look for these plays:

PLAY LIST

DOUBLE PLAY—A play where the fielding team is able to make two outs on one batted ball. This usually happens when a runner is on first base, and the batter hits a ground ball to one of the infielders. The base runner is forced out at second base and the ball is then thrown to first base before the batter arrives.

HIT AND RUN—A play where the runner on first base sprints to second base while the pitcher is throwing the ball to the batter. When the second baseman or shortstop moves toward the base to wait for the catcher's throw, the batter tries to hit the ball to the place that the fielder has just left. If the batter swings and misses, the fielding team can tag the runner out.

INTENTIONAL WALK—A play when the pitcher throws four bad pitches on purpose, allowing the batter to walk to first base. This happens when the pitcher would much rather face the next batter—and is willing to risk putting a runner on base.

SACRIFICE BUNT—A play where the batter makes an out on purpose so that a teammate can move to the next base. On a bunt, the batter tries to "deaden" the pitch with the bat instead of swinging at it.

SHOESTRING CATCH—A play where an outfielder catches a short hit an inch or two above the ground, near the tops of his shoes. It is not easy to run as fast as you can and lower your glove without slowing down. It can be risky, too. If a fielder misses a shoestring catch, the ball might roll all the way to the fence.

Glossary

BASEBALL WORDS TO KNOW

ALL-AROUND—Good at all parts of the game.

ALL-STAR—A player who is selected to play in baseball's annual All-Star Game.

AMERICAN LEAGUE (A.L.)—One of baseball's two major leagues. The A.L. started play in 1901. The National League (N.L.) started play in 1876.

AMERICAN LEAGUE CHAMPIONSHIP SERIES (ALCS)—The competition that has decided the American League pennant since 1969.

BLOOP DOUBLE—A fly ball that falls between the fielders for a two-base hit.

CENTRAL DIVISION—One of three groups of teams making up a league. These teams play in the middle section of the country.

CHANGEUP—A slow pitch disguised to look like a fast ball.

CLUTCH HITTERS—Hitters who do well under pressure, or "in the clutch."

CY YOUNG AWARD—The trophy given to each league's best pitcher each year.

DRAFT—The annual meeting at which teams take turns choosing the best players in high school and college.

EXTRA INNINGS—Innings played when a game is tied after nine innings.

FORCE-OUT—An out made at a base that a runner is forced to advance to.

GOLD GLOVE—An award given each year to baseball's best fielders.

GRAND SLAM—A home run with the bases loaded.

HALL OF FAME—The museum in Cooperstown, NY where baseball's greatest players are honored. A player voted into the Hall of Fame is sometimes called a "Hall of Famer."

LED OFF—Was the first batter of an inning.

LINEUP—The list of players who are playing in a game.

MAJOR-LEAGUE—Belonging to the American or National League, which make up the Major Leagues.

MINOR LEAGUES—The many professional leagues that help develop players for the major leagues.

MOST VALUABLE PLAYER (MVP)—An award given each year to each league's best player; an MVP is also selected for the World Series and All-Star Game.

NO-HITTERS—Games in which a team is unable to get a hit.

PENNANT—A league championship. The term comes from the triangular flag awarded to each season's champion, beginning in the 1870s.

PINCH-HITTER—A player who enters the game to hit for a teammate.

PLAYOFFS—The games played after the regular season to determine which teams will advance to the World Series.

RELIEVER—A substitute pitcher.

ROOKIE OF THE YEAR—An annual award given to each league's best first-year player.

RUNS BATTED IN (RBIs)—A statistic that counts the number of runners a batter drives home.

SIDEARM—A method of throwing where the level of the arm is below the shoulder.

SLUGGERS—Powerful hitters.

SURE-HANDED—Unlikely to make a fielding error.

VETERANS—Players who have great experience.

WORLD SERIES—The world championship series played between the winners of the American and National Leagues.